The Bridge to School

Entering a New World

LIZ WATERLAND

Stenhouse Publishers
York, Maine

Stenhouse Publishers, 226 York Street,
York, Maine 03909

Credits: *page 14:* two stanzas from
'St. Martin and the Beggar'
reprinted by permission of
Faber & Faber Ltd
from *The Sense of Movement*
by Thom Gunn.

ISBN 1-57110-020-2

First published 1994 with the title
Not a Perfect Offering
by The Thimble Press, Lockwood,
Station Road, South Woodchester,
Stroud, Glos. GL5 5EQ

Typeset by Avonset, Midsomer Norton,
Bath, England
Manufactured in the
United States
of America on acid-free paper

99 98 97 96 95 8 7 6 5 4 3 2 1

CONTENTS

Foreword

Fiction, imagination, research notebooks, tape transcripts, photos, and volumes of scholarly studies: the mix intrigued and at first puzzled me as I started to read Liz Waterland's story as a piece of teacher research. As omniscient narrator, she knows the fears and hopes of the teachers, of the young children first entering school, and of their parents. As Headteacher of this school, she knows her characters, and she includes herself among them. As inquirer, she has observed and listened especially closely, recording events in her notebook, on tape and in photos that she researches – looks at again and again. She uses imagination to extend her understanding beyond what she has seen and heard. 'No one can record the exact truth about feelings, not even his or her own,' she argues in her Preface. Effective teaching, she believes, depends upon our understanding how children see and experience school. 'We watch and listen and think and wonder, taking our notes and our photos but, in the end, it is only by constructing the world the child experiences within our own imaginations that we can make that world better.'

As we are increasingly called upon to teach students from backgrounds unlike our own, this kind of understanding is especially crucial and at the same time especially difficult to come by. Liz Waterland takes us beyond the distressing behaviors of four-year-old Rebecca and her mother, into their school fears; and behind Paul's outward withdrawal, into his engulfing memories of abuse and threats from his mother's former boyfriend. All the scientific research studies in the world may not connect us with these students; and without connection, we cannot truly teach.

The initiation into school brings up anxieties not only in children but in their parents and their teachers. What will school be like? Will my child succeed? Will my teaching succeed? This moment is only partially understood when viewed from the perspective of any single participant, for the event itself is the coming together of all participants and what it means to each of them. In her 'imaginative reconstruction' Liz Waterland takes us on an artful tour through the experiences of child, parent and teacher as they interact – an ecology, if you will, of the first months of school.

When I grasp those experiences, I know something different than what statistics about parents' backgrounds or what attitude surveys about school entrance would tell me. I forget the facts and figures, but the experiences stick with me because in some way I have lived them, they become part of me and inevitably change how I see.

They also make me aware of what I don't see and don't understand, and what, therefore, stands in the way of my teaching. Martin Buber, speaking about the dialogue that is education, emphasized the teacher's responsibility to experience his teaching 'from the other side,' to feel how it is affecting the student, to teach not just from himself and his idea of the pupil but 'from the pupil's own reality' (101). This reality is what Liz Waterland's research seeks to reveal.

I envision her desk heaped with notebooks, tapes, photos, and studies by other researchers. The bits and pieces mean little until the researcher interprets them. Waterland has interpreted her data not by analyzing and categorizing and comparing it with other studies but by what she calls 'fictionalizing,' 'an imaginative recon-struction' that extends below the surface of what she has observed into the felt experiences of children, parents and teachers. This is a book about listening with our imaginations, not to fantasize and move us away from reality, but to move us deeper into reality: the reality we cannot see and research in the usual ways. It is about imagining what *does* exist but is inaccessible to our direct vision and so must be envisioned.

There are ways of knowing other than reason and experiment, that is, what we usually think of as 'science,' as scientists themselves attest. 'If you want to really understand about a tumor, you've got to *be* a tumor,' writes researcher June Goodfield, who 'suggests that, for the practice of scientific research, "the best analogy is always love." The reward of discovery is the feeling that "one has touched something central to another person, or to a subject, and one feels silent and grateful" ' (Keller 1985, 125). 'The ultimate descriptive task, for both artists and scientists,' says biologist Evelyn Fox Keller, 'is to "ensoul" what one sees, to attribute to it the life one shares with it; one learns by identification' (1983, 204).

A researcher's methods must be judged in relation to her purpose in making a particular inquiry. Waterland's purpose was 'to understand better the experiences the school offers its children, parents and staff as they approach and begin the new school year.' And her aim in writing up her research was 'to try to tell you what it felt like to be doing or saying whatever the story is about, not just what the doing or saying was.' Her methods of imaginative reconstruction and artful storytelling are beautifully suited to her purposes. 'A fiction is not something untrue,' James Hollis reminds us, 'it is something made (from *facere*)' (6). Like any research account, this is a made thing. Unlike most, it is made of images.

Liz Waterland's use of imagination is rooted in a strong conviction of its importance: 'the road to hell is paved with lack of imagination.' What she means is elaborated by critic and writer Benjamin DeMott, who has argued that America's 'problems are traceable largely to obliviousness, habitual refusal to harry private imaginations into constructing the innerness of other lives' (12). 'My humanness depends,' he insists, 'upon my capacity and my desire to make real to myself the inward life, the subjective reality, of the lives that are lived beyond me. . . . Human growth stems from the exercise of our power to grasp another being's difference from within' (93).

How might such exercise of imagination reform the educational system or, more within our power as individual educators, humanize our classroom and our school? As Liz Waterland's little story with large implications demonstrates, there are no simple answers to school problems. Viewed from within, there aren't even simple problems with clear-cut villains and victims: everyone in her cast of characters is trying to do the right thing in the face of inner and outer obstacles, and often misses. But there is a way, if we have the courage and compassion to imagine.

Glenda L. Bissex

References

Buber, Martin. 1965. *Between Man and Man*. New York: Macmillan.

DeMott, Benjamin. 1969. *Supergrow: Essays and Reports on Imagination in America*. New York: E. P. Dutton.

Hollis, James. 1994. The better angels of our nature. *The round table review*. 1(4).

Keller, Evelyn Fox. 1983. *A Feeling for the Organism: The Life and Work of Barbara McClintock*. New York: W. H. Freeman.

——. 1985. *Reflections on Gender and Science*. New Haven: Yale University Press.

Preface

The Bridge to School is an imaginative reconstruction of
several months in the life of our school. I wanted to
understand better the experiences the school offers its
children, parents and staff as they approach and begin the
new school year. This is always a difficult transition, and
it is important, especially with the four-year-olds, to
make it as successful as possible.

I spent three months observing, and recording what I
saw in words and pictures; listening, and recording what
I heard on tape, paper and in memory. I then re-created
my research as a story unfolding month by month. So
this short book is a work of fiction. That is to say, none
of the characters, except, I think, myself, actually exists
(and I have certainly re-created myself for the purpose).
The research is fictionalized because I wanted to try to
tell you what it felt like to be doing or saying whatever
the story is about, not just what the doing or saying was.
The people who became the characters are real enough,
and so are the things that happened and became the

beginning, middle and end of the story (although not necessarily in that order). They have become my imaginings because no one can record the exact truth about feelings, not even his or her own.

I have arranged our story as a florist arranges flowers, attempting to make them look natural while adjusting balance, colour harmony, height and width; that is what happens when you bring nature indoors to look at it. You start with practical things like scissors and vases and end up squinting with your head on one side wondering whether to move the daffodils to the back so that they can be seen better. Picasso said, 'Art is the lie that tells the truth.' Tease that one out, flower arrangers and researchers.

My scissors were the observations that cut out bits of the day-to-day life of my school. The vases were notebooks, a camera and memory. After that it is all artistry and imagination: throw away this bloom, move that one, add a twig or two.

Research as flower arrangement? An art that lies to tell the truth? Cracks that let the light in? There are so many metaphors, so much to imagine.

Note to the North American edition

The organization, terminology, and language of schooling varies from country to country. There are also variations on the local level. Readers in North America may find the following information helpful.

In funding and status terms, our school is the equivalent of an American public school. We cater to children aged four until seven, at which point they leave our Infant school and go on to the adjoining Junior school where they stay until they are eleven and enter Secondary school. Children start school the September after their fourth birthday in the 'Reception' class.

We are allocated a 'Catchment area,' a list of those streets from which children will have a right to a place in our school. If, after admitting these children, we have unfilled places we may accept children from outside the area. This leads to a certain amount of competition between schools to fill any non–catchment places . . . and when you know that schools are funded largely on pupil numbers (about £1000 per pupil) you see why.

The school year begins in the first week of September and ends in the third week of July. In between there are three terms, Autumn, Spring and Summer. The first terms ends two or three days before Christmas, the second begins in the first three or four days of January and ends just before Easter, and the third begins two weeks after Easter and ends in July. Each term is split in two by a Half Term holiday, a week's break. The total legally required teaching days are 190 per year. (Teachers must do five extra training days as well.)

We invite all parents to have a look round the school when they come to register their child. Not all do, but many accept this first visit. Then, when children are accepted, they have two more pre-school visits. During both of these visits they spend a morning in their new classrooms with their new teacher and friends. The adult stays with the child the first time and meets me, the Headteacher, during the morning. For the second meeting, adults are encouraged to leave the child for the morning. Before the children go off for the summer holidays, we give them a Play book containing drawing paper, stories and pictures about the school and the staff. This is to help them keep school in mind over the next six weeks and to give children some activities for the break.

Then, in September, for the first week of terms, only those children in Years One and Two start school. Reception teachers spend this first week visiting the homes of every child who will be in their class. In the second week of term the new entrants start school for half a day only (excluding lunch time) and this continues for about three weeks or until we and the parents are quite sure that the child is happy, settled and ready for full time. The children then begin for the full day. If there is any doubt about the child's readiness, we offer a further period of mornings plus lunch time only. By half term (last week in October) usually every child is full time, although some continue to go home for lunch.

Because of this long induction (and some children are already familiar with school through older siblings or through the Local Authority Nursery, which is attached to the school) children settle very happily in school, even though they are so young when they begin. I would do the same, however, even if they were much older on entry. It is worth every moment.

June

June brings tulips, lilies, roses,
Fills the children's hands with posies.

You would know a good deal about the school and its area if you looked at the local paper's city map and noticed the names of the streets round the school: Jubilee Street, George Street, Palmerston Road. Rows of Victorian terraced houses with some seventies' council building and, further up, towards the new townships, some very recent private building, raw new bricks and what the agents call town houses ... today's terraces.

The road goes under the railway bridge at one point. It becomes darker and there is often a puddle in the road which sometimes floods enough to stop traffic on really wet days. There isn't a pavement under the bridge and you have to step carefully into the road and round the puddle; cars and lorries don't expect people to be walking under the bridge and so they are an extra hazard; not many pedestrians walk along there. Except when the

Fair is held on Fair Meadow three times a year, then the traffic and the puddle have to give way to the crowds.

When Rebecca came under the bridge for the first time it seemed like a tunnel of huge dimensions. She stopped and looked up to its dripping walls and the strange green bricks; the noise of her feet was trembling among the wet spaces and tumbling back down to her, a long way away and yet still her own. Pulled along, she felt her mother's distrust of the bridge and the wetness. Her mother thought she was frightened of the traffic sweeping round the roundabout to mow them down but Rebecca knew it was the bridge. She knew, after all, what cars could do; like strangers, they took you away to a place where you were dead, but what did wet bridges threaten?

That bridge was the start of school for her. Even when they walked out of it onto the pavement again, past the Co-op and up the little road, it had begun the new thing and not well.

'You go through the bridge and then out on to the straight bit. Rebecca. Listen.'

Her hand was shaken but so was she and she felt only the tug of the familiar hand and the arm which ended in the face that was her mum.

'One day you can do this on your own. Listen because of the traffic. Will you listen? Listen to me.'

Rebecca looked up but her eyes were sleepy and her ears were too shocked to let her eyes wake to her mother's urgency. What would she do on her own? Tomorrow? One day? What day? Two more bedtimes and then the noises and the wet?

When? Mum? When? But it was too late for the answer
or even to listen to the question any more. Sometimes
they could stop and look in the paper shop for a comic or
a bag of crisps (but not sweets) or sometimes it was
possible for them to go round by the church path to stop
and see the children playing at the place where they
played called a school. Today it was the school path.
Rebecca watched and saw . . .

. . . Paul, who was crouched down with his head close to
the brick wall at the end of the playground.

If you bend down very low and look by the corner of
the wall there is a hole. It has a little little head in it with
little little sticks that wave about and then the head comes
out and it is an ANT. Does it live in the hole or does the
hole lead to the ant's house? This time it has a bit of dust
that stuck to its sticks and it waves and waves to get it
off. If an ant sits still it can clean them with its front paws
and then the dust drops off. The little hole is for putting
a twig in that will pick the ant up and then it can walk
along the twig and if you stand up it wobbles and falls
off. Bend down again and put the stick there for it to get
on again. You chase it and put the stick there again and
then it gets on. It falls off again. But if you put the stick
in the hole it . . . it can get bigger. I can dig it and the dust
falls out of the hole in a little pile. The twig breaks. Get
a better one. Dig it out and see the sandy bits that fall out
of the brick with a bloodsucker on it. I saw a bloodsucker! The bloodsucker is red that is how you know it
is a bloodsucker and it is round and it has little little legs

all round it and if you get it on you it will suck your blood and then you die. The stick touches it and the bloodsucker has gone down the hole. The ants will look out because that's how it lives by sucking ants' blood so it has to be very small.

If you sit on the wall you can stop people running along it and then they get cross and push you and you tell them you got a bloodsucker and it will suck them dead. Where? You may have to bend down and see my hole in the wall and my pile of sand. In there it is and the ant is just going in again.

Perhaps the ant is frightened when it goes in and then it meets the bloodsucker in the long tunnel and it is dead. Dead like Fluffy. Fluffy was dead because the car hit her and she didn't know not to run out in the road. Let that be a lesson to you. Let that be . . . that Fluffy is dead and the blood came out for the bloodsucker. Kill the ant and then the ant blood comes out too.

On the front door it says,

HEADTEACHER: Mrs E. WATERLAND

(Perhaps I ought to join the ranks of those who put their Cert. Ed., B.Ed. (Hons.), M.A. on the headings. 'Pure marketing,' one such said, 'and none the worse for that.' But it still looks a bit pretentious, a bit un–primary-school-ish. Degrees teach older children, anyway.)

Now, do I write 'she' or 'I' for the purposes of this story? It is difficult to carry off the voice-of-the-author genre, and the quality of my writing is not something I am sure enough of. But, after all, it is me, and I may as well be honest in the absence of any convincing argument against it. 'She' is an easy person to hide behind, 'I' is upfront, open, valid. Let us, by all means, say 'I'.

I am watching through the window of the cloakroom.

There they are down by that corner again. If they go on digging away much more, the bottom brick will probably fall out. Still, when the playground is tarmacked, the hole will probably be filled in anyway. I do hope they will agree to put in the hills we wanted; the old humpy bit where long-ago concrete set in a strange half-moon shape, perhaps from spilling out of a broken and rained-on cement bag, gives the children so much pleasure just jumping and running. But will it compensate for the loss of the little hole in the wall? Perhaps I'd better specify some hole to be left, just big enough for a twig to go in. Well, the chances of the resurfacing are fairly low so we can worry about that when the time comes. I am told that we can have the mobile reroofed or the playground made safe, but not both. Flooding or falling over; a difficult choice.

I go out on playground duty every week. Parents who complained that their child was being knocked senseless by others found it reassuring that the Headteacher was visible sometimes. One parent had chosen the school because of it, or so she said. A strange reason but as good as the one given by the parent who chose it because we still have school milk or the several who had fallen out with Him Up The Road and thought that their child's

problem would be left behind if they came to a new
school. A fresh start is a persuasive proposition. If the
children could have left their parents behind up the road,
we might have had a better chance.

I remember Andrew, though, who came with a
reputation slightly to the right of Genghis Khan but who
settled beautifully once we'd discovered that he loved
sewing. Perhaps that's it ... Sewing as a Means of
Behaviour Control. An ideal subject for M.A. Research.

The clipboard doesn't work, incidentally, as a tool of
observational research. All it observed was ridicule and
rudery. Probably this was all the fault of that spoof
inservice leaflet in the staffroom.

*Course no. A40897 for Heads and Deputies; Walking
Briskly Whilst Carrying a Clipboard. One of the most basic
skills of Management. Practical Workshop Session. Please
wear comfortable shoes.*

It led to echoes of David Frost, too. When I went into
the classroom Jean said, 'Hello, Good Evening and
Welcome' ... that did indeed both date us and take me
down enough pegs to look for a little notebook that was
less conspicuous. Oh, and the tape recorder and the
camera. 'The observer changes that which is observed'
and I'm not at all surprised. How ridiculous the whole
thing begins to seem after a while; pretence that we can
get to the truth when we are such distorters of the
experience.

★

Every day that little girl and her mother have been here looking down the steps towards the playground. A potential customer, no doubt, about four-ish, and getting used to seeing the school first. A Ladybird Book of Starting School piece of advice which I wish all parents took. Well, I shall meet them soon enough.

It's a serious thing, this taking parents round. Marketing the school, as one of our governors calls it, gaining another £1000. First glimpse, often, of the child and of the things these parents will be worriers about. The ones who want to see the toilets, the ones who ask about class size, the ones who ask about school uniform. None of these are things that really matter once you get talking. I suppose parents need a starting point, because in the end they reach the real concerns if you are clever enough to spot the dropped comment or anxious glance.

The parent at the top of the steps has a very anxious look. I wonder about her, about her name, her child and her anxiety.

Her name is Carol, Rebecca's mother.

Rebecca watched the child by the wall. What was he doing? Would she have to do it? 'What is he doing, Mum?' but Carol hadn't seen him ... or at least had seen him but not noticed him. No answer. She was looking, rather, for the adult. There was a teacher out there every day and sometimes the children came up to her. They seemed to like her, the faces turned up to talk and even, sometimes, listen. Sometimes the lady bent down and talked right into their faces. Sometimes the finger pointed or shook. She remembered when a finger like that made her shake.

'I hated school, me. No good at it, you see, and always in trouble for something. One teacher, he had a pneumatic finger we called it. Drove it straight into your chest so you had to walk backwards to the wall and then he had you. *Don't. You. Ever. Do. That. Again.* And you bite your lip, don't you, to stop the tears.' (Carol made that a statement, not a question, never doubting that I, too, would have shared that humiliating experience.) 'Crying. You never survived that. Rebecca cries and I tell her, you better not do that there or they'll laugh at you. But it's different. Now. Isn't it?'

'Look, Rebecca, you see the lady? That's the teacher in Big School. You mind her or you'll get it.' Oh, God. No. Not to frighten her so soon. 'She looks nice, though, doesn't she? We'll see her soon maybe.'

Carol took her small daughter's hand again and pulled gently. The little girl liked to stop and see the children playing when they came past. It took her mind off the bridge. Every time she hung back at the bridge, frightened of the traffic. Well, her mother thought, so she should be frightened of the traffic.

'When I was small we lived in the country. Played in the road every day and no harm done. Can't imagine it now, can you? I say to Rebecca, don't you go on that road. Daren't let go of her hand. Daren't let her out of my sight.'

That was a good thing about the school. Tucked away out of sight and no roads passing it at all. It looked small and safe. 'A little school for little children,' the Headteacher always said. No big boys in the playground and corridors and, so she'd heard, proper classrooms with doors. Safe and secure.

'We'll go down today, Rebecca, and see about you starting. Hold the rail down the steps and mind and behave.' The steps were steep. When the baby came there would be a tussle with the buggy. But it'll all be a tussle then.

Rebecca concentrated hard on the steps. They were difficult. She held on to her mother's hand and the rail with the other hand, watching her feet and feeling the cold brass rail running smoothly under her fingers as she went. Because she wasn't looking at the playground, she missed seeing Sarah. Before, when they had come sometimes, Sarah had caught her eye. A square little girl with dark hair and eyes, Sarah wore a wonderful coat, a recent birthday present. Her friends admired her coat and so did her teachers. What was it like?

Cherry red, new, and with a full skirt and gold buttons. If you touch it your fingers slide over the stuff and there is a thread on a buttonhole you can twist round your finger. There are thirteen stitches on the round bit there and six buttons and holes to match. If you get your finger on the hole and the button in the other hand and then you push the button up to the hole and then . . . you have to twist it and it comes through, just a little bit of it and if you catch it you put your fingers round the other side and then they pull it through and then it's another five. Only I can't do the top ones, Mrs Cruickshank. I can't do my buttons. They're real gold and the coat is red. If you stroke it it's all cold and smooth.

Rebecca saw the coat first and the child afterwards. A smiley girl and the teacher does your buttons up.

This time, though, because of the steps she missed seeing the sorrow. It was a puddle and the rough edge of the playground. The letter to Sarah's parents apologized and explained that the school was waiting for the playground to be resurfaced. The fall was an accident and the general assistant had done her best with the coat. It was Sarah we couldn't do our best with.

'The poor child's inconsolable. I told her the coat would clean but she just goes on about how she's not allowed to get it dirty and her mum will be cross. Can you see Mum after school and explain what happened? Is it Mum that comes?'

If you rub the mud with your hanky it just gets more and the dirt spreads and then your hanky is dirty, too. You want to go home. You want to go home. The lady, the tall one, bends down and takes the coat away. Your hanky wipes your eyes and then someone says now it's all over your face too. 'Oh, Sarah, come here, let's sort you out,' she says.

My coat, my coat, my coat, my coat. And then, suddenly, there's blood, hurting somewhere. I fell over and hurt my knee and my coat is all hurt, too. Coats hurt with dirt on red; people hurt with red on dirt. I'm not to get dirty, I'm not to get dirty.

The lady has a jumper with a picture of a cat on it. When you sit on her knee you can put your face against the cat. Look! It's all furry, like a real one.

'Feeling better, pet? Don't worry. We'll put some magic cream on that knee and then Mrs Waterland will write to Mummy and tell her it was an accident. Do you like my pussy cat? I knitted it specially to cheer up little girls who'd had a fall over. You stroke him; he likes that and then we'll wipe your eyes and blow your nose. Big blow. There. All better?'

Who'd think a child could get in such a state about falling over? It was the coat of course. A shame with it being her new one.

Sarah showed off her plaster when she got back to the classroom. Mrs Waterland had been in the office with a lady and a little girl. It was the first time Sarah had seen Rebecca but Rebecca remembered Sarah.

'That's the coat girl,' she told her mother urgently.

'What, what do you mean? She does talk nonsense sometimes.'

Desperately, Carol wished she was less easily embarrassed. It was school and all the feelings she hardly recognized except for the effects they had on her, the blushing, the talking and, oh, worst of all, the tension over what her daughter might say. It made her unfair, she knew it did, and hated the voice that emerged from her tight, dry throat, the nagging, fractious voice that made Rebecca look at her with fear and uncertainty and tightened the health visitor's mouth.

In the evening of that same day, at home, I am reading for my dissertation.

MULTIPLICITY OF CAUSATION

Perhaps the most fundamental of all is the fact that
rarely, if ever, are either problem behaviour or
learning difficulties due to one single cause or
circumstance. Rather there is a multiplicity of
interrelated and interacting factors, so that there is
unlikely to be a short cut to either diagnosis or
treatment. The health, appearance, intelligence and
whole personality of the child; the economic, social
and cultural standing of his parents; the relationship
between them and all the other members of the family;
the child's experiences at school and in the
neighbourhood – all these and many more factors
may play a part. Their combination and impact are
unique for each child. Thus the relative importance of
a particular set of circumstances differs for each child,
even in the same family. (Mia Kellmer Pringle, *The
Needs of Children*, Hutchinson 1986)

So do I feel better for that? How to resist the feeling of
despair that such information engenders? What on earth
can I, therefore, *do* about it? There is only me, a few staff
and this multiplicity of factors; it hardly seems a fair
contest. Stop picking on me, you big bully Multiplicity
of Factors, pick on someone your own size. What can I
do with a multiplicity of factors times 209?

I need an antidote or I shall think that I am omnipotent
. . . or supposed to be. Even the children think I am. What
can I do about Fluffy and the coat? Even the knee will
heal anyway and it's the cream that's magic, not me or

even our general assistant (her jumper has powers, though). There is a poem that provides comfort for such moments when a headteacher is in need of magic cream herself.

(Is it cheating to put two huge quotes into the same chapter of a dissertation? It'll put the word count up satisfyingly. Well, as Mr Barnes told me for A-level, quote only if it is relevant. Yes, indeed, Douglas Barnes, author of *From Communication to Curriculum*, Penguin 1976, for it is he, taught me at my grammar school and told me I could write if I tried and so is responsible for much, was responsible for this quote, too, since he suggested that we start keeping an anthology of our favourite poetry. I shall never forget the disappointment in his voice as he realized that half of us had included 'Softly along the road of twilight'. Nor shall I forget the way he became tired of my insistence that it should be *my* communication that shaped that day's curriculum and told me, bluntly, to Shut Up. Well that's the risk you run when you start ideas up with children . . . sometimes it doesn't go the way you want.)

From 'St Martin and the Beggar' by Thom Gunn:

[Martin, a Roman soldier, newly converted to Christianity, meets a naked beggar one pouring wet night. He cuts his cloak in half and gives one piece to the beggar, keeping one for himself. Later, at an inn, he meets the man again and discovers that it was Christ in disguise. Christ speaks:]

'You recognised the human need
Included yours, because
You did not hesitate, my saint,
To cut your cloak across;
But never since that moment
Did you regret the loss.

'My enemies would have turned away,
My holy toadies would
Have given all the cloak and frozen
Conscious that they were good.
But you, being a saint of men,
Gave only what you could.'

That is magic cream; remember that we need give only
what we can. We may never make saints but we may stay
sane. So, maybe, will the children. Ask only what they
can give, also. Parents, too, come to that. I thought about
the mother I had met that morning and sensed again the
delicacy of her bridge to school, the fear at crossing it.
What had she felt, seen, wondered about?

Carol came to the door and saw the notice, handwritten
in bold school writing, WELCOME, and then a lot more
about caretakers and visitors report to doors. The door
was on a spring but it closed slowly enough for you to
get in without hurrying. Several doors, one with a notice
on it: PLEASE COME IN.

There were two ladies in the room, obviously an
office: computer, telephones and filing drawers. One,

smiling, said 'Can I help you?'

It was just that feeling of shyness, of not being allowed to be there and having to explain yourself to the lady. She pulled Rebecca forward, more roughly than she meant to, and the other lady bent down, 'Hello, have you come to look at our school? What's your name?' Carol waited, tensely, for the inevitable. Rebecca hid behind her and put her thumb in ... again. She did show you up when she did that. Anybody, the doctor, the health lady, even the library. Grabbing hold of her arm she tried to pull the child forward.

'Say hello to the ladies, Rebecca.' Shamefaced, she looked up. 'She always does that, I don't know why, noisy enough at home.'

The feeling of failure again. Not her fault this time, not like when she had failed her eleven plus, but her daughter now. Even at four, already can't do the right thing. Carol's fingers tightened on her small daughter's arm. Shake her. No, not here or Rebecca would howl and that would make things worse. What will the ladies think?

The first lady looked at Carol. 'Do you want to register her? Is it for school or nursery?'

For a moment Carol panicked ... a different difficulty; something else to worry about. You could see the fear flit across her face.

'How old is your little girl? We'll know from that. It is rather complicated, it all depends on her birthday, you see.' Well, she could cope with that and then the ladies would make the decision.

'She's four, four in April.' Please, Rebecca, come out

from behind me. Look at least half intelligent.

'School, then, in September. Do you live in our area?'

'Just on Victoria Road. The other side of the bridge, is that all right?' Was that the right thing to say? Was that the right answer?

'Oh yes, that's ours all right. Would you like a look round the school while you're here? See if you like the look of us?'

The lady was smiling again. Carol wondered what to say. Was the lady busy or did she mean it? It would be nice to look at the place but who was the lady? She hadn't said anything about her name. Rude, I'd call it, not to introduce herself.

'Yes, please, but not now if you're busy ... we could come back ...'

You could hear a lot of children coming along the corridor; not noisy but rumbling and twittering. A teacher called out, 'Rosey, don't push, please. Quietly, children, or we'll turn round and go straight back.' The noise stopped at once. That was good. Discipline. That was what Rebecca needed. Make her talk when she was spoken to.

The lady said, 'It's nearly dinner time so the children will be clearing up but if you don't mind that, you're very welcome to look round. Shall we take down the details first and then you can decide?'

Rebecca was looking round now. Not quite so close to Mum but still holding on to Mum's coat. The noises were strange. And the feet and a door banged. There was a bird singing. Did they have a bird? Mum's coat is blue and there is a little tear.

Ambiguous, that. Did I mean tear as in rip or tear as in weep? More uncertainty. What did the child see as she peeped round her mother at me on her first visit? No, not her first visit. I recognized her as the one who often stopped at the top of the steps with Mum to watch playtime. The Ladybird-reading mum. Poor woman looks worried to death; expecting again, I'd guess. The child is shy and yet interested, a charming combination. Beware the terrified and the overconfident equally. Boredom will drive her out from behind her mother as we fill in the form; *name, age, date of birth, address, telephone (if applicable)*. 'If applicable' is a tense sort of phrase. Let's try 'if any' next time.

Sure enough the child, Rebecca, (another one), is edging out to look at us properly. The tear or tear is not so interesting as the shaggy toy dog in the corner.

'That's Pudge. He looks after the children and they look after him.' When they come in roaring or terrified to be comforted or told off, or when it is just too much to bear, whatever it is, and I may never know, then Pudge is for cuddling or hitting or whatever makes a child feel better. He's a good friend.

'Can I hold him?' she says and for a moment I wonder what Mum's reaction will be. She is scandalized at the child's boldness.

'Rebecca! That's the lady's. Put it down.'

I have to smile. Does she think it is my own personal cuddly for when life gets too much for me? I pick Pudge up and reassure her that it's all right. 'He's for the

children.' The 'lady' isn't so bad after all, that's what I
hope she's thinking. She'll go home and say to Rebecca's
father (there is one, is there?), 'She was a nice lady. Had
a big toy dog for the kiddies and let Rebecca hold it. Ever
so nice.' Still being ever so nice, I prepare to take the two
of them round school if they would like a look?

'Well, no, not now. We can come again, another time,
but it's dinner time and Rebecca's dad he gets home for
dinner while he's on shifts.' Yes, yes, of course. No
problem. In fact, better really since I can be prepared and
have the tour script ready. Here's the library and our
lovely big hall. Will your little girl/boy (delete as
applicable) be having a cooked dinner, have you decided
yet?

Carol signed the form and left it on the desk. She took
the big floppy dog out of Rebecca's arms; not roughly,
just certainly, and took her hand again.

'Thank you, thanks. I'll come in again and see round.
Thank you.'

Rebecca trotted beside her, looking up at her mother.
Well, that was done. At least she hadn't disgraced herself
and all the form was easy to fill in. Even Rebecca hadn't
cried. Relieved, Carol looked down at her daughter.
'Shall we have some crisps on the way home?'

Fancy that lady never saying her name. Rude.

Rebecca bent her head suddenly. Crisps, yes. But then
it was the bridge again. And every day. Bridges are hard,
whether you are going under or over them.

July

Hot July brings cooling showers,
Apricots and gilly flowers ...

She never had gone back for a look round. The next
week Dave was at home and he hadn't wanted to go to
the school, not at his age (joke). After that the moment
seemed to have passed. She'd have to ring up, or go in
again and think of something to say, to start the
conversation off, without a form to do this time.

Still, in the end it hadn't mattered, after all. The school
sent a letter and it told you when to bring Rebecca to see
the school and for parents to have a cup of tea with other
parents and meet the Headteacher, Mrs E. Waterland.
Was that the lady they met?

'You're going to school today. To see the lady again.
And some other children. Good job your yellow dress is
clean and try and keep it clean then it'll do for Grandma
on Saturday.'

Please Rebecca, be good. Don't let me down. Talk to

the lady and do as you're told. What if she doesn't like it,
what if she runs away? There was a boy who did a runner
from a school in the local paper, knocked down just
outside the gates. Did they lock the doors? How did they
stop the children running away? Rebecca ran after her at
the playschool once but she hadn't got out of the
building so she took her back. But she wouldn't be there
all the time and it was further and there was the bridge
and the traffic. That front door hadn't been locked.

'Listen, Rebecca, you're to stay when you go to school
till Mum comes for you. You're not to go out on your
own or the cars will get you under the bridge, do you
hear?' Frighten her. That'll stop her running off.

Rebecca looked up, bewildered, at her mother. For a
moment Carol cursed herself. There, now she'd put the
idea of running off into the kiddy's head. She shook her
arm, gently. 'Do you hear, only with Mum. Or Dad.'
She added the afterthought without much conviction.
Still, after the baby came he might just have to take or
fetch sometimes. Suppose the baby wanted feeding at
home time? Surely he'd see that? The trouble was Dave's
mum and dad. Mum did the children and home, Dad did
the work. Well, he'd have to help. After all sometimes
you saw dads taking children to school or home just out
in the street; people did nowadays.

If only starting Rebecca at school was going to make
things easier.

The day that the new little ones come in for their first
visit is always difficult to manage. They are invited to

spend the time in their classrooms with their new teachers and classmates. The logistics of this are complex. The current occupants of the classrooms have to be found homes and teachers from somewhere, and when your school is fully occupied without so much as an empty cupboard to spare, this is not easy. The problem is solved by choosing the day that the Year Two children have swimming and games and so are out of their rooms. Then the present reception children can use the mobiles (complete with leaking roofs) and the supply budget can take the strain of supervision. The extra worry is, of course, that such frivolous use of supply money might see us short when a real need arises, a staff epidemic of stress, for instance. We run the most depressing risks in education these days.

Their second visit is easier because the Year Twos go up to the junior school and that leaves room for a game of musical classrooms without such problems. Come the day, then, there is mass evacuation, lacking only the labels, 'Please look after this child.'

'Children, I want you all to listen to me, please. Stop what you're doing and listen. Listen. Mark, that means you as well, are you listening? No, you're not, you're talking. Thank you.'

With varying degrees of effort, from ramrod-stiff, arms-at-the-side attention to one eye still on the computer screen, the children stopped what they were doing.

'It's time to start packing away for dinner now. *When*

I tell you, Karen, not before. I want all the tables cleared and the chairs pushed in. Then sit on the carpet ready.'

Sarah and Paul were at opposite ends of the room. Sarah had been colouring in her picture of the princess to go with her story and Paul had been sharpening his pencil, earnestly, into a rapier point which would snap again as soon as he tried to write with it. Both knew the time had come to stop. Paul blew the shavings out of the sharpener and put it back on the teacher's table. He looked critically at his pencil. That was the best point he'd managed all day. Save that one. He put the pencil carefully, and against rules, into his tray. Pencils were supposed to go into the pot for anyone to use but he had worked hard on that and no one else was going to have first go. Already he could anticipate the way he would touch the pencil on the paper to make a black, clear dot before, with a sudden jerk, the point would give and a tiny spray of lead would mar the sharpness of the dot. You drop dead with lead poisoning if it gets in your blood.

'Paul, sweep up the pencil sharpenings you've left, please.' His second favourite job. Smiling, Paul wrested the dustpan and brush away from Penny who was sweeping spilt sand.

'Mrs Cruickshank says I've got to have it now.' Penny gave up without a struggle and went to sit, rigidly upright, arms folded, chest nearly bursting as she thrust it upward to show how ready she was.

'Well done, Penny, you did get cleared up quickly!'

As for Sarah, she was delaying the process. Just

another minute and the lace on the princess's dress would be finished. Kneeling on her chair, back turned towards the room, she coloured frantically, elbowing her protest as Robert tried to put the coloured pencils in the tub. It was no good, it was spoilt. Robert had jogged her arm and the colour had gone outside the lines. She surrendered the pencil to Robert, thumped him half-heartedly on the shoulder and took her book to Mrs Cruickshank. 'Look at my princess.'

'That's nice, Sarah. I like the lacy bit round her dress. Put it away now and come on the carpet.' Sarah looked at the picture as she walked to her tray. Mrs Cruickshank never noticed the bit outside the lines.

'Now, children. As you know, you're all getting too big to be in this class any more.'

'I'm five.'

'Yes, Tommy, I know, and so next year you'll be Year One children and be in a new class. Your teacher will be Mrs Dane.' At least that had finally been settled after all the staff discussions about who would have Year Two next year.

The children looked at each other in exaggerated delight and with noisy ooh-ing and ah-ing.

'I like her. She's all right.'

'I'm sure she'll be pleased to hear that, Paul, I'll tell her.' Occasionally, the temptation to a little irony, or even sarcasm, became too great. She really shouldn't do it, though, well aware that it was wasted on young children and resented by older ones.

'Well, you're going to spend tomorrow in her class so

that you can meet her and get to know each other. My new little ones will be coming in so that I can get to know them too. And now, look, there's Mrs Samuels. You'll be late for dinner. Who's ready?'

At once every child sat up, as Penny had, arms and legs folded and expressions of agonizing virtue and readiness on their faces. The ritual began.

'If you're a packed lunch, you can go out. If you're a dinner, go to the toilet and wash your hands.'

The next day was what the school called, oddly, the Push Through. Year Six children in the juniors went to visit their new secondary schools and that left room for a chain reaction of children moving on: Year Twos to go to the junior school, reception children for their first classroom visit. It was a strain. You never felt comfortable while you were having to be all sweetness and light with your new children. Jean never felt settled with a class until she'd had her first row with them. And this class's next row would be this afternoon. Who had left all that sand on the floor?

After dinner, the little girl, self-aware in her yellow dress and white summer sandals, stood waiting. She had come in the door and there was a lady that Mummy said she had seen before but there had been a fluffy dog then and he wasn't there now. She couldn't remember the lady but she remembered the door and the way it closed behind her very slowly as if a person you couldn't see was shutting it with a click behind you. It had made her jump again, that little, secret click. She walked along a long carpet with little squares, one foot in each square until she bumped into a table. Mummy tapped her head and said, 'Look where you're going.' How did she know where she was going? Blindly she followed, unaware that her mother was following the lady until they came to another door. Near the door was a toy cooker and a saucepan, like the one at playschool. Tentatively, Rebecca put her hand out and touched the knob. She looked up at Mummy, but she was listening to a lady. Rebecca opened the oven door and looked in. There was a dolly inside. Why was the dolly in the oven?

'Mummy, there's a dolly in the oven, Mummy. Look.' She reached in and took the doll out. It was old, with strange, harsh hair sticking straight up and no clothes on. There was felt pen on her tummy. Rebecca pulled her mother's skirt. 'Mummy. Look.'

Something hurt me! Something hurt me!

The child staggered under the thump of her mother's hand to the side of her head. There was a roaring voice that said something.

Something. What had it done? What had the voice said? It was a dolly who hurt me. I done it wrong. I done it wrong again.

The yellow dress was spotted with crying.

Ashamed, Carol looked down at her daughter. She had wanted to do it right with the lady there and now it was all spoilt. Rebecca had been naughty and now she had lost her temper in front of everybody. What would they all think of her and of the child?

Slowly, so as not to stand up too soon and show her

face, Carol bent down and picked up the doll. Gently the lady took it from her. She said it didn't matter.

The lady bent to Rebecca and turned her face up to her. While Carol was fumbling in her pocket, the lady produced a tissue and wiped Rebecca's eyes. Appalled at such an invasion of her privacy, Rebecca recoiled from the pink paper and buried her head in her mother's skirt, the familiar smell better than this strange place and the doll that hurt your head when you touched it.

'I'm ever so sorry,' Mummy was saying, 'she isn't usually so naughty.' Had she convinced the teacher? Holding the doll awkwardly the teacher opened the door.

'Come on in and meet your friends, Rebecca, and your new teacher. A bit of an upset, I'm afraid, Jean, but this is Rebecca and her mummy.'

Another lady bent down to see the little wet face and the fright. Her eyes flicked up to see the parent standing just behind and she nearly laughed at the similarity of expression. Both ashamed, bewildered, out of their depth. An experienced teacher, she recognized equal need.

'Why not just come in and watch for a while before Rebecca joins in?' she said gently, indicating a small chair at the side of the room. Thankfully, Carol sat down and pulled Rebecca to her knee. She buried her face in the shining hair, smelling of Vosene, and the other smell, Comfort, came from the clean yellow dress.

Rebecca looked up at her mother and felt the tension drain away a little. It wasn't so frightening for her mummy now. Sniffing still, she peeped at the big room.

School, not playschool, something different, but still some children and some tables and some chairs and some grown-ups. There was a table with painting. Rebecca enjoyed painting. Did she dare go and see? She touched her mother's face, twisting round to see her reaction. 'Can I paint?'

As she came up to the table one of the ladies smiled at her and held out a papery sort of coat. 'You'll need an apron, Rebecca. I'll help you put it on.' The coat thing seemed to be the apron, and Rebecca turned round and held her arm backwards towards the sleeves. Alarmingly, the adult held the apron in front of her. 'No, you put it on frontwards, look, to keep your tummy clean, not like a coat.' The red apron was very strange. It went on and you had to put your arms in front of you to put it on. At playschool you put one, blindly, over your head. Rebecca looked down at herself and felt the lady pulling the neck firmly and doing the apron up behind her. Shyly, Rebecca said thank you. She glanced towards her mother, who smiled at her. That was all right, then.

(Sensible, those big aprons. Perhaps she'd be all right now. Carol looked round the room for the first time, less anxious now that no one was looking at her.) Jean watched, from the other side of the room, as the child picked up the paint brush.

You pick up the brush. Red first. Hold the brush up and the paint runs off it in a thin stream of colour, back in the pot but you have to wipe the brush on the pot to stop the drips on the table. The playschool lady told you that. Wipe, carefully, once, twice. Paper is white and clean. Put your brush on it and pull it, it goes over the paper. The little brushy bits stick out like a fan and the red comes in a thick smooth line with the hairy edges. Slowly down the paper, watch the line coming and the hairy edges spread down. Stop. Pick up the brush and dip it again. Wipe. Once. Twice. Just a little drip from the end on the paper. Drop. Touch it with the brush and the drop joins the brush again. If you push the brush straight down it all spreads out like a hand with fingers and then you get a round bit. Swirly round and swirly round. Two rounds and a line. You put the brush back in the pot and then another colour. Yellow. Pick the brush up and wipe. Once. Twice. Put the yellow line exactly over the red one and it goes another colour, not red any more and not yellow but there is still red on the edges and the thick bit of yellow is sitting on top of the red and you can see the brush has gone red and the new colour, called ... called oranges. An oranges line with red and yellow bits. If you wiggle your hand the brush wiggles and then the line wiggles. More paint. Blue. Wipe. Once. Twice. Dots. Dot. Dot. Dot.

The voice surprised the child as she bent over her paper. 'What a lovely painting. Can you tell me about it?' Rebecca didn't look up. Stopping making dots she whispered, 'I done oranges.' The adult bent lower. 'Sorry, I couldn't hear you.' Defeated, Rebecca shook her head and stood back. Pulling ineffectually on the sleeves of her apron, she tried to take it off. The hands which belonged to the voice helped her and, freed, she went back to her mother.

Jean cursed herself. Just the wrong thing to do with this one. 'I'll put your name on it so you can take it home, shall I?'

'Answer the teacher.' Her mother poked Rebecca on the shoulder. 'Go on. You got to talk to her when she says. Say thank you.'

Jean saw the small fingers twisting the hem of the yellow dress and smiled. 'It doesn't matter. Look, I'll put your painting on the heater to dry. Don't forget it.'

For a while Rebecca stood and watched until, enticed by the jigsaws, she ventured to another table. 'Mum, come and do this one.' Carol got up and followed her. They sat side by side and, once again, Jean was struck by how alike they looked as they bent over a Postman Pat puzzle. Neither spoke. Jean waited until the puzzle was finished and then came over.

'Mrs Adamson. Would Rebecca stay here while you go to the hall for coffee and the meeting? We'd come and fetch you if she was upset.'

Carol looked uncertain. Rebecca was started on a Mickey Mouse.

'She stays at playschool now,' she said doubtfully.

Going up that corridor on your own without Rebecca to be the reason and then that big hall and there were some chairs she'd seen. Where did you have to sit? Who did you have to talk to? Could she bridge the gap with whoever sat next to her?

'All right. You'll be all right now, and be good.'

Rebecca was pleased with the jigsaw. You put the bit

with Mickey Mouse's ear in and then it's finished. Run
your hand over the picture and you can feel the pieces all
fitted together and rough but no spaces so you know it's
done. Tell Mum.

The trouble is that when you are doing a jigsaw you
have to concentrate and you might even hum a tune
called 'Postman Pat' so you don't hear what grown-ups
are saying to each other. They never told her, just each
other, and she didn't know that Mum had gone and that
was why she had said be good. She meant be good while
I'm gone like she used to say at playschool but then she
always left at playschool. You didn't know she had gone
this time. Or where. Or why.

'I want to go home. I want to go home.'

Recalled from the hall, in front of everybody, Carol
was mortified by her daughter's screams. 'I'm ever so
sorry. She isn't usually like this. Do stop it, you silly
girl.'

'It doesn't matter, Mrs Adamson. Honestly. Lots of
children find it hard when they first visit. Just stay with
her for the rest of the time and she'll be fine. Won't you,
Rebecca, now Mummy's here again?'

Exhausted, the child sat and sucked her thumb on her
mother's lap while Carol rocked her daughter slowly to
calm herself and to let her embarrassment ebb away.
What they must think of her! All the other children
playing so nicely and the mums in the hall looking at her
when the teacher came to fetch her out because Rebecca
was being such a baby.

Well, she was just a baby, anyway. Only four. Carol's

expression of tension and blame softened as she thought how little her daughter was. Her own baby and the new one on the way. No wonder, poor little toad. Well, September was a long way off yet and that headmistress said that the kiddies would start for just two hours at first until they were happy. Not so bad, maybe. She stroked Rebecca's hair.

'We'll go home soon, Baby Bunting, and you can take your picture to show Daddy, shall you?' Baby Bunting meant forgiveness. The child relaxed.

On the way home they stopped for some sweets. 'Don't expect these every day you go to school, though, will you?'

Rebecca carried her painting, rolled up, to show her dad. She looked up at her mum. 'Mum, I didn't get my dress dirty, did I, at school?' It never occurred to her that she would have to go back.

Preparing for these parents' meetings is no fun. Each year I think that I must remember to keep the notes I make so that I don't have to make them all over again. Each year I put them away safely and each year I can't find them. There must be a safe place somewhere with years of notes in them.

Extract from THE HEADS' LEGAL GUIDE, page 1/95
[There are five pages of explanation of the regulations on reporting to parents including the following:]

The Parents' Charter, published by the Government in

September 1991, undertook to ensure that parents had
access to up to date and objective information which
would facilitate their choice of school and enable them
to keep in touch with the schools their children attend.
In pursuance of this policy the *Education (School
Performance Information) (England) Regulations 1992* (SI
1992 No. 1385) which revoked the 1991 Regulations
(SI 1991 No. 1265) on school performance, require:
a) More performance information in school prospect-
uses and governors' annual report to parents, and
b) The publication of comparative tables of school
performance.
The regulations are explained by DFE Circular 7/92,
*The Parents' Charter; Publication of Information about
School Performance in 1992* which supersedes Circular
9/91.

So every year at this time I update the school booklet
for parents to take account of all the information the
regulations require me to put in. This year the major
change is to include the number of unauthorized
absences for the previous year. We don't have any
unauthorized absences since, at infant age, absences are
authorized by the parents, if not by us. Does 'There were
no unauthorized absences during the last school year'
sound good for the school or not? Do parents realize that
it is in response to regulations that we put that
information in? It does seem peculiar to do so, otherwise.
It is almost as though we started boasting that we had no
unauthorized killings, beatings or robberies either. You

should see the authorized ones though!

The school booklet is ready for the first parents' meeting. Their children are in their new classes and we provide coffee and a buffet prepared by the school meals service. Trying not to wonder what will happen when our school meals budget is delegated to us (the temptation to go for packed lunches, taking the money and running, may be too strong), we encourage as many children to have a cooked dinner as possible, and as many parents to apply for free meals as can do so. I don't mind if they have the meal or not; we need the money for special needs that it brings us.

Ten o'clock is the time for the meeting, after the children have settled in their classes. The first parents begin to arrive. Some I already know; they have older children. Eight years in the school means that I know many of the families well, several of this year's intake I remember being born. In earlier times being The Old Retainer, knowing all the families well, was a good aim for a headteacher. Now it leads to wondering, should I think about moving on? Am I still effective, fresh, efficient? Did Miss Read worry about such things?

The parents I don't know hesitate by the door, wondering where to sit, whom to talk to. I find this hard too. What is the right note for these first-time meetings? Jolly, warm, friendly; cool, distant, calm, The Headteacher? What is she? I never get it right and always feel awkward, unsure of what to do while people come in. If you talk to those you know well it seems clique-y, if you don't it's stand-offish.

Finding something to do is best. I go round handing
out the booklets. Brilliant! I can say something to
everyone and have to move on. Remember that for next
year too.

Gradually the chairs fill. This is the meeting we can
assume will be well attended; all those anxieties to be
dealt with means a good turnout. Once they and the
children are well settled, next term, they will come in
alone or with a friend to talk about specific worries, but
such a mass response seldom happens again.

Have I arranged the chairs well? A circle, more
friendly than straight lines, with no special place for me.
I sit where there is a space. Very democratic and relaxed
and a good thing too. I think, as I often do, about Miss
Fincham. She was a previous head here and, by all
accounts, formidable. Talking of her, the caretaker
smiled. 'Miss Fincham? Well now, she was a Lady.' I,
plainly, am not. It was Miss Fincham who would allow
no undressed doll in the Wendy house and whose neat
writing in the school logbook solved the problem of
what the children should call the nursery nurses by the
quaint formulation of Miss plus their first name. Miss
Catherine and Miss Mary held sway all through the
Fincham years.

The stories are many, especially from ex-pupils, and
all contrive to make me feel sloppy, inadequate. If she
ever held parents' meetings, I am sure all her chairs faced
the front in rows.

We begin. Welcome everyone; introduce myself; offer
my credentials (a parent myself, of course); go through

the information in the booklet, picking up points as they occur and trying to guess the thoughts going through the mothers' minds (no, no fathers at all this year). This part is as brief as I can make it since they can read it for themselves when they get home, and I know that I talk too much when nervous.

The rest of the meeting is for questions. Will they ask about performance indicators, absences, SATs results, complaints procedures, the content of the curriculum, the arrangments for sex education and religious instruction? All these must by law be in the prospectus. My experience is that none of them has any influence on parents choosing an infant school. When I take parents round, they remark on the absence of big boys in the playground, the displays and books round the school, the fact that children mostly wear uniform, and the size and use made of the school grounds. For this meeting I deal with the following concerns, none of which appears in the regulations:

- head lice, prevention of;
- bullying, incidence of;
- PE kit, need for;
- happiness in children, promotion of;
- reading at home, importance of;
- school dinners, quality of.

This last is a wonderful natural break. The buffet, prepared as a promotion by the Catering Service and our marvellously obliging school cook, is ready. 'Come and see for yourself.' At this point Anne, Jean's nursery nurse (no Miss anymore, I am afraid), comes into the hall. Could Rebecca's mummy come back to the classroom? The poor woman gets up, scarlet, and everyone looks at her. A naughty child? A wet child? A sobbing child? The smugness is palpable; their child is managing without them. The food is a welcome distraction.

What have the parents thought of me, and of the school? One child has been crying and the parent has been sent for. Rebecca's mum. She was one I have seen but cannot picture yet, or give a family name to. This is a real worry. Parents expect me to know their names, often coming to see me with no preamble at all. 'Her coat's gone missing.' I don't know whose mum she is, let alone where the coat is. I can remember all the children, however, and that seems to please parents. One parent told the governors that she chose the school because when I took her round I knew and greeted every child we saw. We joked about a few planted children.

Was the tone of the meeting right, I wonder? People go off at last and the hall is cleared. Damn! I forgot to go and see about the distressed child; Mum looked fairly distressed herself. Too late. They've gone home. A chance for some reassurance has been missed. I must try and spot Mum on her next visit to see if the child is happier.

In my diary I note, 'See new mum re crying child.' Their next visit will be next week. Then the home visits in September before the children start part-time. We really are trying to get this right.

September

Warm September brings the fruit,
Sportsmen then begin to shoot.

The holiday has bridged the gap between old and new. The school is clean, scrubbed from the top of the walls to the bottom of the urinals. The cobwebs on the high windows are gone, the drips behind the sink where the paintpots are washed have nearly vanished, only a faint pink stain shows that red pigment is particularly difficult to shift. Always, it is the pink stain that stays round the cuffs of infants unskilled at rolling their sleeves up. No doubt, in a hundred and seventy homes, even the cuffs are clean as new uniforms, shoes and haircuts are lying in wait for the first day.

The great pleasure of teaching is this fresh start each year. Clean school, new children, new plans and ideas. This time all will be well; this term will be straightforward, clear of illness, oil leaks, vandals and staffroom grumbles. Hope is what teachers have a real talent for.

Three or four days to go. Staff have been in at various times in the last week or two, but today I am on my own. The caretaker has finished and has left me to lock up in a sort of Gray's Elegy mood. Not a good metaphor, strictly speaking, of course, since an elegy is an ending and this is a beginning. It is appropriate, though. I am sure that years ago there wasn't this tinge of melancholy, like the stain of old red paint, lingering into the new term. I'm either getting old or there is something in headship that produces a sense of lowing herds winding slowly o'er the lea, a distinct feeling of plodding in the air as the school is left to cleanliness and to me. The school is such a wonderful place without any children in it; we are the teachers with the most talented and successful classes and the most tidy cupboards in the world until the children arrive. Yet, still, we hope every year that this time it will be true even after they appear.

It makes me smile to think that here the staff are, hoping in our small corners, and there the parents are, hoping in theirs. What are they hoping, I wonder? That shoes will stay polished, shirts white and children out of trouble, no doubt. Perhaps children have this effect, of hopefulness, on all adults that contact them. That is a child's great talent, too.

Well, well. Time to lock up and go. Nothing more can be done until term begins.

During the first week of term we don't bring any reception children in. Instead, the class teacher and her nursery nurse spend the week home-visiting, talking to parents, meeting teddy bears and baby sisters, drinking cups of tea, admiring curtains. I worry sometimes that it all might seem patronizing, lady of the manor-ing, snooping, even. I think how much it relies on the skills of the staff, to do it well, and they certainly seem to succeed. When we asked parents to tell us what they thought of the home visits, all were enthusiastic. They liked the privacy to talk about their children, the chance to know who the teachers were and what they would be like, the chance to introduce their child to the new adults on familiar ground.

(This is important. 'What happens if you go with strangers, Kevin?' Never, never go with strangers. Strangers will kill you, they give you poisoned sweets and take you to see their puppies in haunted houses where they will do unspeakable things to you and you will never, never see your mummy again after you have been locked in a cage to be made fat and no bone on the floor to trick the witch with while Gretel thinks of a plan. There might be a wolf down in the Co-op or a Freddie down the street who will smile at you but his nails are like knives and forks. Never, never go with strangers. Except this stranger in whose hands Mummy will leave you for the next five hours while she goes away. What a bewildering world it is.)

Then, the children come in part-time at first, just mornings or afternoons. We never seem to get this right. We balanced the two sessions by shortening the morning to two hours because we got complaints. 'She's had longer in school than my child.' We did it first by starting

later in the morning, to give parents time to get here
without a rush. But some had older children to get to
school by 8.50. We could hardly send them home for an
hour. Then we tried one week of mornings, one of
afternoons but there were complaints that the children
(never the parents, of course) got confused. In the end we
decided to do what seemed best to us and hoped that
most people wouldn't mind.

This year, then, it's morning from 9.00 to 11.00 or
afternoon from 1.15 to 3.15. Two adults in each class,
the class teacher and her nursery nurse, me around as
needed and only small groups at a time.

A nightmare of organization with home-visit appoint-
ments, part-time teaching groups, dinner supervisors to
arrange. This must be better than everyone in at once and
for all. A retired teacher told me about forty-five
reception children, straight from home, no nursery or
playgroup, and crying, some of them, for weeks as a
result. There are worse nightmares than ours.

That first day was dreadful, for a start off. Rebecca got up
all right and put on her new uniform. It was nice that the
school had uniform, making it a bit special for the
kiddies. She didn't want any breakfast, though, and was
ever so quiet. Even when Dave got out the new rucksack
he'd bought for her she wasn't what you'd call thrilled,
said thank you nicely, though. Carol was afraid that
Dave would be cross with Rebecca for not being thrilled
enough but he was all right about it. Said that she'd
bound to be a bit nervous, first day, and she was to have

a lovely morning and tell him all about it when he got home.

Dave had seemed more interested in Rebecca starting school since the teacher had come to the house and he'd been home off shift. Talking about it, he'd thought it was good that the teacher had come for a visit, and he'd liked the chance to explain that they'd been a bit worried about Rebecca's ears because of all the infections she'd had. Carol was sorry that she hadn't thought to say that herself but she'd been so anxious that Rebecca should behave properly and that the teacher would think her nicely brought up and good. It was always the same; something got in the way of her thoughts when she was faced with teachers and school.

Dave managed much better. He was plain and straightforward, she'd always liked that about him. When the new baby had been born he'd been wonderful about the things you had to do, registering and all that, and now he was helping and so proud of the little boy. They called him Mark. A good baby, thank heavens, and Rebecca seemed to like him. It was bad timing, Carol knew, with Rebecca starting school, but you couldn't think of everything.

For now, it was enough to worry about getting the child to school on this first morning.

On the way it got worse. Rebecca started dragging back, which made walking so tiring and difficult. Then the tears had started. By the time they got to the bridge the little girl was crying uncontrollably and Carol was virtually dragging her along. Thank God that Dave had stopped at home to look after Mark for her, else she wouldn't have been able to manage at all. Taking Rebecca by the shoulders, Carol bent down and shook her daughter.

'Listen, Rebecca, you got to go to school. You'll like it ever so much when you get there and you're just playing up.' As always, anxiety made her voice shrill and disagreeable, but at least the shaking made Rebecca stop shrieking. She settled down to a steady and irritating sobbing as they went into the dark shadow under the bridge, the child held firmly by the wrist, dragging her feet, and the mother, tight-lipped and harsh, hating herself and the morning.

At the beginning of the path by the church the little girl in the bright red coat that Rebecca talked about was standing patiently while her mother adjusted the straps on a pushchair in which sat a chubby toddler, the image of her sister. Carol couldn't get past so she waited just behind. Rebecca, tear-sodden and exhausted, recognized the coat too, and put her thumb in while she watched.

Sarah's mother straightened up and then realized that she had been holding up the traffic. 'Oh, I am sorry,' she said cheerfully to Carol as she wriggled the pushchair aside. 'Do you want to get by?' Carol smiled uncertainly. 'New, are you?' the other mother asked and the two began to walk on, keeping pace with each other.

The little girl's mother seemed very unsure of herself, and the little girl had been crying, that was obvious. Her mum looked as if she'd be crying, too, in another minute. 'Sarah, say hello to the little girl. What's your name, pet?

Rebecca. That's nice. Say hello to Rebecca, Sarah. Sarah'll look after Rebecca, won't you? She's ever so motherly. Lovely with Jade, that's our youngest. We've had such a terrible holiday. Jade's had chickenpox and Sarah was sick all last night. Her dad had her this weekend and it's always sickness after that. Too much junk food and late nights. It's all right for him; she never starts till she gets home. I thought I'd keep her at home today but she wanted to come. You should have heard the fuss! It's good, isn't it? My mum always says that we used to batter on the doors to get out; nowadays they're battering to get in!'

It is by such things that we are healed. The steady, friendly voice chattering on calmed Carol and took her attention from Rebecca. The tension eased and she found herself nodding and smiling in reply. Beside her, Rebecca had stopped dragging and was walking alongside plump little Sarah. After the first 'Hello', obedient to her mother's commands, neither Sarah nor Rebecca had spoken but both were eyeing each other and Sarah was noticing with interest the new patent leather shoes the other wore. 'Your shoes're shiny,' she remarked kindly.

The steps gave Carol her chance to be friendly. 'Let me take your little girl's hand while you do the pushchair,' she said and felt pleased when Sarah took her free hand and, both feet together, jumped down the steps beside her. Rebecca, more uncertain, held the rail as they went. At the bottom Carol felt even more pleasure that Sarah did not immediately let go but continued to hold her hand as they crossed the playground between the crowds of children and parents to wait by the cloakroom door for it to be opened.

There is the ritual jangling of keys as the caretaker opens the doors. 'Morning, everyone,' he says, as always, and, as always, a variety of children's replies as the first ones push in. 'Hello, Mr Cross,' 'Mr Cross, I'm six now.' He always answers cheerfully, interested, popular because of his jokes and his patience with spilt water and wasted paper towels. This morning you can tell the new mothers. Uncertain, they wait to find labels on pegs, relieved by the sight of the class teacher and the emptying of the cloakroom as the older children, before their coats stop swinging on the pegs, disappear into class.

Sarah does not wait to say goodbye to Rebecca. She and her mother, who gives a quick reassurance as she goes, 'Don't worry, she'll be fine,' disappear to tell a less than thrilled class teacher about the sickness in the night. Carol and Rebecca wait for Jean to show them Rebecca's peg. There is a curious feeling of calm about them both now as they stand among the other newcomers. Close together and united by both fears and, for the first time, anticipation, some sort of bridge has been crossed.

These first few days of the new year are hard for us all, staff, children and parents. It is a time when the school feels like a collection of many different souls rather than the one community it will become in a few more weeks. The little ones are still only part-time and so have to be thought about separately. Letters home must be got to them earlier and they are missing at dinnertime. The afternoon children are not in assembly and so will have to get used to it all later when they finally join us, and parents appear at odd times of the morning to collect them. It is all very unsettling. The older children, too, are still not quite established. Learning different routes from new classes and new ways of working if they have changed teachers, they are both excitable and unsure. This year we have not had to rearrange classes, however, and so friendships and company are continuing.

As for the staff, there is an air of relaxation because the tiredness is still in the future but the new classes are challenges to be accepted as fast as possible and this causes a certain nervousness. Children you have only met as playtime hooligans and thought you hated have become human, and the dear little child who was so friendly when passing in the corridor has already turned out to be an attention-seeking nuisance. It is unsettling and difficult at first, and there is the knowledge that for a while none of the children will be provided for with the subtlety the teacher knows she will be able to plan for in a week or two when she understands them better. Hand on the paperwork, my colleagues, but the child is the only real record of herself.

I know Sarah and Paul already, of course. It is no surprise that Sarah is beaming up at me as she bustles the dinner register importantly up the corridor. We chat about her holiday and her sister for a moment or two before she says, in a perfect imitation of her mother, 'Well, I'd better be getting on' and continues on her errand. A good, competent child. What a treasure!

Paul I am less happy about. He has come back fractious and withdrawn from us in a worrying way. Such a self-contained little boy last year, this year he seems to be brooding and sullen. I watch him at playtime. He stands by the wall, just in front of his interesting hole, but he makes no attempt to see if his beloved ants are still there. He watches the others and doesn't move. In class his teacher is concerned about him, too. He hasn't settled and is a source of constant ripples and unease.

Gradually, Paul began to shuffle, still sitting cross-legged, you'd be hard put to say how, still watching his teacher, until he'd moved several feet across the carpet from the isolated spot he had chosen first. Now he was just behind Hannah. Pat watched him out of the corner of her eye while she went on reading the story. This one she hadn't got to grips with yet. Jean had said he was a lovely lad but so far he had only been a pain. A new class was always an upheaval for the children but she was puzzled by the difference between what she had heard about the child and what she had met.

Paul sat upright and apparently innocent as Hannah suddenly squealed, turned and punched him. 'Mrs Dane, Hannah hit me for nothing!' Outraged, Hannah began to cry. 'He pinched me, Mrs Dane, he pinched me.' 'I never!' Pat, with infinite patience, shushed them both. 'Not another word from either of you till I ask you' and she began the tedious business of trying to get the truth out of small children. Claim and counter claim, accusations, mainly from those who couldn't possibly have any idea of what had happened, who were the other side of the group, tears and lies. All of the class were relying on her for justice; if she could not offer it, there would be another reason not to trust the grown-up world.

Eventually, with a leap of faith that she had got it right, Pat pronounced the verdict. Hannah had indeed punched Paul; that was obvious, but she had been provoked. Paul, on balance of probability, had pinched the little girl. Therefore, he was to be sat on his own on the naughty chair, a social outcast far from the storytelling. Hannah was told, yet again, that it was not right to take the law into her own hands.

The formula came fluently. 'If you had told me that Paul had pinched you, you would have been good and he would have got told off; now you are in trouble, too, because you hit him. You must not fight back, Hannah. Do you understand?' Pat looked at the children and wondered again what the point was of the determined efforts they made to prevent retaliation. Half the children had been told to fight back by their parents and the rest got the same message from the TV anyway.

'Now, can we get back to the story, please? Where were we?' A mental note made to discuss Paul with Jean and Liz at playtime.

His mother came to tell me that he hadn't wanted to come back to school and still said he didn't want to. She couldn't get anything out of him at home. Could I try? Perhaps he was being bullied and was frightened to tell. You hear a lot of that goes on in schools. I promised to have a word with Paul and see what I could find out. Sometimes a child will talk to a teacher because the emotional investment is less and the teacher can keep calmer than a parent. It is never easy, though. What can this be? There had been the child who was frightened because the cistern was making a strange noise; the child who had been stealing crisps out of lunch boxes; the child who had lost her shorts and was frightened to tell. It is hard to tease it out, often, and needs imagination to construct fears from the half hints and inadequate explanations offered by children who sometimes don't know what the trouble is themselves. How much they rely on our ability to imagine it better. I am not prepared for this one, though.

'It's the man in my head. He won't go away. He's there all the time and he's going to get my mummy. He said he would and he's got the key and it's my fault because I told and I told Mummy and it was Mummy and he ... he was ... and he hit her and he. And he said he would and it's because of me and the locks and they can't get him and he's in my head. I try ... I try and do my work and he is in my head and I think about him all the time and he ... he ... he is in my head. It hurts my head. He hurts my head. He hurts and it's Mummy. They don't know where he is and he's here. Please tell them.'

The little boy is inconsolable. His nose running

ribbons, and crying in great gulps and frantically gasping for air, he sits on my lap and judders out some dreadful story that I can make no sense of. All I can do is wait until the terror has passed far enough for me to question him.

'Paul, who is the man? Tell me about him. No one is going to hurt you.' [Oh, the certainties we lie with.] 'Tell me about him and we can help you.' [Oh, the certainties we lie with.] It took a long time but slowly I find out about the parts of Paul's life that are unimaginable to me and that no one had told me about. I find out that Paul and his brother had told their mother that her last boyfriend had treated them with great cruelty whenever they had been alone with him. She, in a new relationship, had at once told the police. Paul had spent much of the summer holiday, when my imagination had pictured him at the seaside or playing happily in the garden, giving evidence on video for the abuse proceedings to begin. In the meantime, the man had disappeared, no one knew where he was and the police, Paul knew, had been unable to find him. Kindly, his mother had promised him that, if he told the police all about it, they would catch the man and put him in prison so that he could never hurt the boys again. But they hadn't, had they? And somewhere out there was a man who had promised, in God knows what demonic circumstances, that, if Paul told, he would come back and get his mother. The man had a key to enter the house but he hardly needed to. He was already deep inside, in Paul's head. Every night he crept around in there, every day he put his hand over Paul's eyes and said, 'Guess who?' Unable to sleep or work or play, the child was possessed by the fear of his secret visitor.

And no one had told me. Not the mother, nor the police, nor the social services had thought to let the school know what this little boy was involved in. Did his mum really think it might be bullying that was the cause of his unhappiness? That Paul had had no problems coming to terms with the experiences of those weeks?

'Why didn't you tell Mummy about the man in your head, Paul? She wouldn't let anyone hurt you, would she?' It is hard not to let the tears well up when a five-year-old answers a question like that by saying 'I didn't want to worry her.'

I ask to see Mum and her new boyfriend. They are nice people, and both have come to the school often to see Paul in the concerts or talk about his work. They are genuinely upset when I tell them what Paul has told me and the reasons why he kept quiet about it all.

Mum shakes her head. 'I really thought he had got over it and had coped with it all,' she says and I believe she really did think that. The idea that children get over things easily is very strong. A dead pet? Get another and they'll soon get over it. A stay in hospital? Buy some sweets and they'll soon get over it. Divorcing parents? See daddy once a week and they'll soon get over it. The road to hell is paved with lack of imagination.

I can't tell you how the story of Paul ends, even in my imagining. He went for family therapy for a little while but then the council rehoused them after the new baby was born and they moved away. Perhaps I could pretend to know what has happened to him since but, paradoxically, while it was lack of imagination that I blame for his misery, I can't bring myself to construct him any further now. It would insult the truth of his bravery. I do sometimes wonder if he has ever found another ant hole to crouch in front of and study. If you know of a better hole, go to it. The joke being, of course, that there is no better hole; this is all we have.

Later on that day Sarah's teacher stopped by my filing cabinet where I was trying to guess what I had filed something under so that I could find it again. She was carrying a pile of children's work and picked one out. 'Look at this,' she said, delightedly. 'What a joy the child is!' I love it when staff share their joys as well as their troubles. This school is good at that; we are positive thinkers on the whole and love the children's efforts to struggle through the world of education.

STORY BY SARAH age 5 and a hrf.

DRAGON ISLAND

can you spot the giaant's Bird's In my picture? Now I will start the story one day me and my brthe and my sisder and my frend went to dragon island the giant Bird's Brort us there and we killed the dragon's seesd the giant kild the pirates and us and the salu's floow home on the giant Bird's.

One gets adept at reading these lovely offerings. After a while there seems no real reason why we do not put

'Br' and 'the' together to spell brother or see and sd for seized. (The computer does not agree, however. Spell-check recognizes none of Sarah's attempts as the word she intended. A teacher of emergent writers plainly cannot be replaced by a computer. What is the old joke? Any teacher who can be replaced by a computer ought to be.) But that wretched apostrophe S! Greengrocers' disease at 5 and a hrf seems a poor reward for the struggle to make sense of the rules of punctuation. I wonder why I can punctuate with a quite pedantic punctiliousness but cannot spell well? Pity the word processor suffering the reverse problem; there is no apostrophe check on this machine. One day there will be, I am sure. Then the debate about the skills we need to teach will be extended even further. Meanwhile, let us just enjoy Sarah's story, apostrophes and all; she deserves it.

Rebecca enjoys writing too. She always did like to scribble and draw; any bit of old paper and a pencil keep her happy. It was a blessing during the long waits at the antenatal clinic before the baby was born and Carol always kept something she could draw on in her handbag. Once, Rebecca had drawn a picture of the nurse and given it to her. The nurse had been really pleased. She was a good girl really, kind and very good with the baby now. Settled into school as well, thank goodness. Sarah was her friend in the other class and Carol got on well with Sandra, Sarah's mum. One day she'd ask her for coffee, perhaps. At the moment it was just passing the time in the playground or when they fetched the children from playing at each other's house occasionally. Still, it was the first friendship Carol had made since they had moved here and she hoped it would develop well. Perhaps Dave would like to meet her, too. He liked Sarah when she came to tea. The sort of little girl that Rebecca ought to be friends with, he had said.

The only worry now was the way Rebecca still cried every morning as they set out from home and at the end of the day. The teacher said it wasn't unusual. 'Lots of children find the first leaving each day hard and most are a little tired and cross after their first few days of full time. And there's the new baby.' Ever so nice when she said it but it still seemed a worry. Why did Rebecca do it? She was fine in school all day, the teacher said, and she seemed to enjoy it. Lots to tell her dad about in the evening anyway. Carol was secretly rather proud that her small daughter chattered so happily about her doings. Not like some. She'd heard mothers say they couldn't get a word about school out of theirs. Dave and she knew all about the new teddy bear in the book corner and the lady who cooked the dinners. It was just the crying at each end of the day. Not frantic anymore, just steady sobs. Tore you up it did.

Getting cross hadn't helped. Dave had lost his temper at first, thinking Rebecca was being a baby and baffled that she wouldn't tell. Then Carol had tried wheedling it out of her but she just shook her head and dropped her eyes in that way that meant you might as well save your breath. Even teacher had tried (what was her name?) but couldn't get anywhere. Well, at least Rebecca is good at school; nothing to be ashamed of there.

One day was a highlight for Rebecca. You had to line up
first. You line up for coats and dinner and to come in
from play but one day it was another lining up. When she
asked the lady where they were going she said 'Music'.
Music is on the radio and telly. Where is the telly? 'Where
is the telly?' But the lady stood at the end of the line and
then the teacher came and said they were all ready. You
had to stand up very straight and not talk and then you
go along the long bit past the playhouse and the dolly
that got writing on its tummy and went in the oven.
(Rebecca turned her eyes away. Jean wondered why the
child never wanted her turn in the playhouse.) You went
past the lots of other children in rooms. The big hall, not
with a front door, is for dinner but now there wasn't any
tables. Teacher took you to a corner place with a carpet
and you sat down. Then another lady came and said
'Hello, children.' Rebecca, shyly, said hello and the lady
smiled at her.

That was the day that Rebecca discovered she could
play the triangle. It isn't an easy instrument for small
children, having an annoying habit of swinging round
when you hit it. Trying to solve the problem by holding
it still results in a curious donging noise that drops dead
at your feet instead of the flying bell notes that ring so
satisfyingly. It is hard not to laugh when I see the little
girl, lip between her teeth, watching the swinging
triangle so carefully and just managing to catch it with
her beater. All there is in her world at this moment is the
effort of making the instrument ring to be the silver bells
for 'Mary, Mary, Quite Contrary' as the wavering

voices join in with their teacher's. Her wrists still braceleted with baby fat, dimples twinkle in and out on her hands as she holds the beater clutched in her fist. Jerkily at first she brings her hand down and up all in a line with her arm, stiff as a drumstick. As she gets the idea, though, her wrist relaxes and the sweetening of the tone of the instrument rewards her efforts.

Watching, I wonder if she will remember this afternoon, the September sun flooding through the huge windows of the hall, and the singing and the triangle?

Long ago, the sun was shining on the floor in big squares and we were sitting, just as Rebecca is now, singing 'Glad That I Live Am I'. On the wall there was a picture of a child, with cropped hair, a calm, blind look, holding a bird carefully in cupped hands. There was a ball on the ground. The long curtains were blowing in the breeze through the window and the shadows were moving over the picture. I remember that.

Years later I found a poster of the picture, Picasso's 'Child with a Dove', and bought it for my childhood's sake. What will Rebecca remember of her time with us? One day, will the sound of another child playing the triangle bring back our school for her, this first small triumph? The past is another country but I do not think they do things so very differently there, after all.

May

May brings flocks of pretty lambs
Skipping by their fleecy dams.

We are still here, except for Paul. All still working together, doing our best, children, parents and staff. The lovely weather of that September has moved on through a cool and damp winter to a showery, sunny May. The school grounds, which are the great surprise of our city school, are foaming with wild flowers, meadowsweet, May blossom, cow parsley, campion, dog daisies. The white season.

Nearly a year after this story began Sarah is still laughing her way through the days; a golden child, good at everything. She has grown out of the red coat and in any case would scorn its babyishness now. Buttons are no mystery any more; these days she offers to tie boys' shoelaces after PE.

It took us a long time to discover Rebecca's fear, which you will have realized at once, of the darkness under the bridge. It was the Billy Goats Gruff that finally got it out of her one evening when Dave was reading it to her; her own troll came out of the shadows then and was butted under a lorry by her daddy. The silly thing was, as Carol said, there was another way they could have come to school all along. It was a bit longer but the baby enjoyed the airing and Rebecca could walk with Emma, her second best friend (Sarah was still the first). It just goes to show that you never know with kiddies. Rebecca still enjoys music and is reading a bit, too. Carol is very proud of her.

Carol and Sandra are good friends. Sometimes they spend the afternoon together while the two little ones play before they set out to collect the girls from school. Sandra tried to get Carol to come on the PTA committee but so far she hasn't got the courage. The baby is a good excuse, anyway.

I often wonder about Paul. We heard from another school that he had been admitted and I passed on all the information I had but that was the last contact. I hope he came through it all and, like so many children, survives. Perhaps they do get over things; how else could most grow up sane?

As for the school, well, we carry on. At this stage in the year the children all know each other and the staff, they walk confidently and have secret jokes. The community has been called into existence by our combined wills; children, staff and parents linked by some vision that we share.

Looking back, I think how far we have come since

September and the beginning of this story. The summer
term is halfway over and already we are planning for our
new intake; the list is finalized, the booklets printed, the
visits planned. It seems neat and tidy, all systems up and
running. We have planned for the children's beginning
to be as good as it can be. Now we can only imagine
what they will make of the first days and weeks of the
new year when they move to new classes or visit for the
first time.

It is our imagination that will make all well or all ill; we
cannot ask small children to make sense of the world of
school unless we have stepped into it with them. We
need to bend our backs to their eye level and wonder
what it is that we see. We need to listen to the voices and
words that children hear as if they are a foreign language.
We need to feel fears and joys that are long lost to us, or
that we may never have known.

We watch and listen and think and wonder, taking our
notes and our photos but, in the end, it is only by
constructing the world the child experiences within our
own imaginations that we can make that world better. I
owe a debt to Rebecca and Sarah and Paul, their parents
and their teachers, although they are fiction, which will
be repaid to their real heirs who will join my school in
many futures.

Booklist

There is a considerable body of research and opinion relating to the needs, expectations and experiences of three-, four- and five-year-olds in school. Most of it reflects the assumptions and viewpoint of the adults involved, but in some cases there has been an attempt at an imaginative leap into the mind of the child. This booklist notes writers who have convincingly imagined a child's perception. North American editions are listed where available, but unfortunately, many books are out of print or hard to obtain.

I have not included the works of 'pure' fiction that have also influenced my thinking about young children. To do so would require me to start with the final chapter of *The House at Pooh Corner*, which I first read aged around five, to Angela Carter's *The Magic Toyshop*, which I am reading now.

Ashton-Warner, Sylvia. *Teacher*. New York: Simon & Schuster 1986. An impressionistic autobiography of a

New Zealand infant teacher, this is the book which first made me question the experiences I offered to children in my classroom and so, perhaps, began this whole study many years and children ago.

Atkinson, R. *Three to Five Year Olds in School: An Approach to Evaluation.* Northamptonshire, UK: Northamptonshire County Council 1986. Atkinson gives examples of questions about little children in school, under a wide range of headings, for adults to ask of themselves. I found this framework very helpful, not only in evaluating our provision for the early years but also in suggesting areas on which children might have views. Like *Learning Now* (see page 70) this paper developed out of an L.E.A.'s concern for early education provision in its schools. There is no doubt that the position of the very young children in mainstream education is recognized as being problematic.

Avery, Gillian. *School Remembered.* London: Victor Gollancz 1967. A collection of reminiscences by a wide variety of adults, famous and unknown, from the fifteenth century onwards. It is depressing to read how often school is remembered with dread or fear:

> This was the feeling which my first year at school gave me, a feeling of being shut in some narrow, clean wooden place; it must be known to everyone who has attended school and the volume of misery it has caused will not bear thinking of. (page 16)

Axline, Virginia. *Dibs, in Search of Self.* New York: Ballantine 1986. The classic account of a deeply disturbed child and his therapy. At first it seems to be entirely a factual transcript of the events that took place. Story-making about these events is integral to most of the book, however, and is sometimes part of Axline's responses to Dibs. She uses her interpretations of what happens as part of the therapy, enabling Dibs to make sense of what is happening. After the scene in which Dibs buries the father doll in the sand tray, Axline tells the story for him. 'The boy rescued his father and the father was sorry for everything he did that had hurt the boy. He said he loved Dibs and needed him.'

Barrett, A. *Starting School: An Evaluation of the Experience.* Norwich, UK: C.A.R.E., University of East Anglia 1986. Includes photographs as stimulus to thought about the experiences of the children. The viewpoint is largely that of the parents and teachers of children in reception classes. No special attention is paid to four-year-olds. Was their perception any different? Like many of the adult viewpoint studies I have read, this conveys an overwhelming feeling of the goodwill with which teachers and parents try to lead children into school, but the black hole is still the difficulty in knowing what the child knows, thinks and perceives.

Berg, Leila. *Look at Kids.* Harmondsworth, UK: Penguin 1972. Again, photographs form an important part of the resource offered by this series of observations of inner city children. Leila Berg has a wonderful ear for

the things a child says that might afford a view into the
black hole. One chapter consists of the recollections
about school of the parents of some of the children she
observed. Again, most were of fear and pain. In the
1960s Leila was the first writer of the *Nippers* reading
scheme, which tried to offer children from an inner city
landscape books to read which would truly reflect the
lives they were leading.

Cambridgeshire County Council. *Learning Now*.
Cambridge, UK: C.C.C. 1988. An attempt, in both
literal and language snapshots, to define the experiences
of children in a wide range of Cambridgeshire schools.
Despite the brief and varied descriptions, there is a
distinct feel of a unifying philosophy, of a tone or
expectation about what education is and what it is for
which suggests, rather than demands, that adults should
look carefully at the coherence of provision for all
children in their schools.

Carr, J.L. *The Harpole Report*. Harmondsworth, UK:
Penguin 1972. A fictional account of a term in the life of
an acting headteacher in a London junior school in the
1950s. No one who went to such a school at that time
could fail to recognize the truth it is based on. It forms an
interesting contrast to Fred Sedgwick's book (q.v.).

Clay, Marie. *Observing Young Readers*. Portsmonth,
NH: Heinemann 1982. Marie Clay collects the research
papers on which she based her publications about
reading and writing in the early years at school. Much of

her work is concerned with wondering what is in children's minds when they see books, make marks or understand print. The observation schedules, tables of figures and descriptions are all directed towards the major problem: what is in the child's mind?

Craft, Maurice, John Raynor and Louis Cohen. *Linking Home and School*. Harlow, UK: Longman 1970. A study, which seems very 1960s-ish now, into relationships between home and a variety of primary schools. Much of the debate seems to be of the past: unstreaming, whether parents should visit classrooms, P.T.A. meetings, parent helpers in the classroom; battles long won. Whether these devices help to solve children's problems seems no nearer certainty three decades later.

Crowe, Brenda. *Play is a Feeling*. Andover, UK: Unwin Hyman 1986. Like Leila Berg, Brenda Crowe has long been a champion of the child in the education system. Here she observes children playing and coping with the demands of adults and asks us to face up to the question, 'How would you feel?'

de Bono, Edward. *Children Solve Problems*. Harmondsworth, UK: Penguin 1972. A different approach to finding out what children experience. Whereas many writers use what children say or do to trigger attempts at empathy, de Bono asks children to draw their solutions to problems they have identified. Some children provide their own commentary but de Bono also describes his understanding of what the pictures show of the child's thinking and of the philosophy behind it. This is often good fun, as in the attempts by children to stop animals fighting. De Bono notes that co-operation seems to be the child's preferred way of dealing with the world.

Donaldson, Margaret. *Children's Minds*. New York: Norton 1979. Chapter 8 of this celebrated study of the way children perceive their world is entitled 'Why Children Find School Learning Difficult'. It is interesting to compare the tenor of Margaret Donaldson's argument with that of, for instance, Piaget, in whose work there is always the impression that failure in children to make sense of experiences is due to deficiency, albeit a natural one, in the child. Here the suggestion is that the deficiency may well be in the experiences themselves. There seem to be two distinct attitudes to small children; one, that lack of maturity causes the child to mistake the world; the other, that the world is asking inappropriate things of the child. My impression is that the latter view began to be prevalent fairly recently, perhaps from about the 1970s. Certainly much work that pre-dates that decade is mainly concerned with how the child can be enabled to cope with the culture of the education system, rather than suggesting that the system needs changing. (There are, of course, exceptions like Montessori and Ashton-Warner.)

Drummond, Mary Jane, et al. *Four Year Olds in School: Policy and Practice*. Slough, UK: N.F.E.R./S.C.D.C. 1987. A collection of papers presented at a seminar in March 1987 which considered the quality and suitability of what Mary Jane Drummond describes as 'the bizarre mixture of experiences that we call education' (page 59) and which we offer to very young children in mainstream schools. Of special interest to me, since my school was involved in her research, is the paper by Christine Stevenson, which describes, with imagination and sympathy, her observations of small children playing and working. Her work and that of other contributors show how often provision is unsuitable for four-year-olds, and in her Afterword Mary Jane Drummond suggests, among many other points, how helpful it would be if the adults involved attempted to look at schools from the child's point of view.

Mary Jane was also chairperson of a D.E.S./Regional Course *Curriculum and Practice in the Reception and Infant Class* (1986), whose unpublished report I, with other colleagues from Peterborough and around Cambridgeshire, was involved in compiling. The report addressed the problems that teachers of very young children faced in their own schools and considered ways of improving conditions for both children and teachers. Sadly, in many cases, the attitudes of headteachers and teachers of older children in the school were seen as a major block to improved practice.

Gardner, Dorothy and Joan Cass. *The Role of the Teacher in the Infant and Nursery School*. Elkins Park, PA: Franklin Book 1965. This study of the interaction between teachers and their children highlights the different expectations in nursery and infant schools in the late 1950s. Detailed transcripts of the teachers' speech are analysed under 79 different categories. One's major feeling at the end of the study is a desire to know more of what the children said in response to the closely recorded utterances of the teachers.

Hadow, W.H. *Report of the Consultative Committee on the Primary School*. Norwich, UK: H.M.S.O. 1931. Despite the title, the report deals only with children between the ages of seven and eleven. However, I have included it because of its unequivocal demand that the school should show 'a single-minded devotion to [the pupils'] needs in the present . . . not what children should be . . . but what, in actual fact, they are' (page xv). More than sixty years later we are still unsure that we can achieve such an aim. Is the ethos of the 1990s becoming one in which the child will again be found wanting if he or she does not cope with the system?

Haggerty, Joan. *Please, Miss, Can I Play God?* London: Methuen 1966. This 'adventure in dramatic play' is amusing ('We can't have them running round expressing themselves all day, can we?'), and the account of the children's responses gives some moving insights into their thinking.

Holt, John. *How Children Learn*. New York: Dell Publishing 1972. I prefer this to John Holt's companion book, *How Children Fail*, because it is less a criticism of the educational system and more an investigation of the children themselves. Notable, above all, for one child's elegant critique of democracy, 'Why is it better for three people to be selfish than for one?' (page 102). Again, the emphasis is on the adult interpreting what he has seen and heard in order to try to explain the child's thinking. It is cheering to realize how good experienced teachers get at doing this and how often it leads to changes in the system as mismatches between our understanding and the child's become apparent.

Humphries, Steve, Joanna Mack and Robert Perks. *A Century of Childhood*. London: Sidgwick & Jackson 1988. Produced to accompany a Channel Four series of the same name, this social history of childhood in the twentieth century developed from reminiscences and interviews. Memories of school are especially lively, such as those of the child asked to copy the word 'abundance' from the board and illustrate it. Not having any idea of its meaning she 'drew three happy little buns complete with currants and blue bows dancing a jig. "Tra-la-la" came a little caption out of their mouths' (page 112). For this she was caned. Seventy years later the sense of injustice is still burning off the page.

Kohl, Herbert. *36 Children*. New York: Dutton 1988. Like John Holt, Herb Kohl is concerned to adapt the system to the child. He is working with much older children but his work shows how important it is to get education right for the child from the beginning. Most of his students had been bewildered from their earliest days in school. 'Alvin doesn't like to talk of this subtle, prejudiced undermining of his pride and confidence. He takes it within, sometimes sulks and comes close to

quitting' (page 212). It is the silence, through inability or
unwillingness to speak, that makes our understanding so
much – in the end and despite what we see – a question
of intuition.

Lev, Mary and Bronwen Dorling. *Rising Five*. Pre-
school Playgroups Association, undated. A modest little
book of suggestions for the playleaders of older children
in playgroups. Its emphasis throughout is on the
importance of the adult's imaginative support for the
child's thinking.

Montessori, Maria. *The Child in the Family*. London:
Pan 1975. Less concerned with the minutiae of
educational provision than much of Maria Montessori's
writing, this was written primarily for parents. It is very
concerned, however, with the pre-school child and in
her emphasis on the need to observe, consider and
empathize with the child's needs, highly relevant to the
teacher of four-year-olds. A chilling passage refers to the
Japanese tale of the spirits of dead children, which,
having ascended into eternal life, work very hard to
build little towers with pebbles. But evil demons destroy
the towers faster than the children can build them. This,
says Montessori, 'symbolically represents the damnation
of the child' (page 50). We are asked, by implication, to
consider what else in a child's experience the story might
symbolize.

Mellor, Edna. *Education through Experience in the Infant
School Years*. Oxford: Blackwell 1950. Edna Mellor was

one of the first advocates of the need to change the experiences children are offered in early schooling so that these may better match the child's understanding. Quoting Froebel, Dewey, Montessori and Rousseau, she argues that, without imaginative entry into the child's mind and emotions, education cannot benefit child or society.

Opie, Iona. *The People in the Playground.* New York: Oxford University Press 1994. Iona Opie visited the playground of her local primary school regularly over a period of twenty-three years. During this time she observed, noted and wrote about the conversations she had with the children, their activities, games and talk. The result is this wonderful book full of childhood. The tender interest she takes in all the playground's many activities is the reason for the open-heartedness the children show to her. Playground Duty will never be the same . . .

Opie, Iona and Peter Opie. *The Lore and Language of School Children.* New York: Oxford University Press 1987. A classic study of the voices of children at play and in private. The songs, games, jokes, social rules and beliefs of children throughout Britain in the 1960s give an insight into some of the ways children perceive and cope with the demands of the adult world they share with us.

Plowden, Bridget, et al. *Children and their Primary Schools; a report of Central Advisory Council for Education.*

Norwich, UK: H.M.S.O. 1967. It is difficult to be objective about a report that is so much a part of the professional background of teachers of my generation. It is equally difficult to imagine such a report ever being produced again in the current climate. Such a time-consuming, detailed and open-minded brief as the committee was given seems now to belong to another world; perhaps, in fact, it does. But the reader has to look no further than the title to realize the report's underlying assumption that schools should belong, not to the state, the parents, nor even the teachers, but to the children; the schools are 'their' schools. Most famously, 'at the heart of the educational process lies the child. No advances in policy, no acquisitions of new equipment, have their desired effect unless they are in harmony with the nature of the child, unless they are fundamentally acceptable to him' (page 7).

Schools Council. *Primary Practice; S.C. Working Paper 75*. London: Methuen 1983. A further attempt to look at what actually happens in the classroom and at how far this meets the needs of the child. Weakened, in my opinion, by an apparent reluctance to consider the infant years in any but very general terms.

Sedgwick, Fred. *Here Comes the Assembly Man*. Bristol, PA: Taylor & Francis 1987. A year in the life of the headteacher of a Suffolk primary school. Sedgwick goes to considerable trouble to emphasize the respectability of his data and the attempts he has made to check their accuracy. In this respect it contrasts with *The Harpole*

Report (see page 70), which is wholly fictional. However, the two books are indistinguishable in the truth they convey to anyone who has been in the position of the authors. I find this an interesting paradox. Presumably, if one has never been in such a position, the unreality of them both would be similar? Perhaps a story can only convey truth to those who share its experiences?

Sims, Mary. *A Child's Eye View*. London: Thames & Hudson 1976. Based on Piaget's model of children's thinking development, this is a detailed attempt to use direct observation and recording of children problem-solving to suggest what a child might and might not understand about the experiences offered at home and school. Strongly mathematical in bias, the study nevertheless has some interesting attempts to consider what may lie behind a child's responses.

Smith, T. *Parents and Pre-school*. Oxford: Grant McIntyre 1980. A report on the Oxford Pre-school Research Project which concentrated on parents' views about how their children respond to the experiences they are offered before school.

Tizard, Barbara and Martin Hughes. *Young Children Learning*. Cambridge, MA: Harvard University Press 1985. The conversations of young children with their adults are recorded and contemplated. What sort of experiences are the children having at home and at school? What does the children's speech tell us about their understanding and growth of thinking? Are the experiences they are having in school the best that can be offered and if not, why not? Provocative reading for any adult advocating that three- and four-year-olds should have access to formal educational provision, the lessons the book offers in listening to the child and considering what we hear as clues to what the child thinks were very relevant to my study.

Tough, Joan. *Listening to Children Talking*. London: Ward Lock Educational 1976. Again, a project based on the words of the young child.

Vallender, Ion and Ken Fogelman. *Putting Children First*. Bristol, PA: Taylor & Francis 1987. A collection of papers and essays produced 'in honour of Mia Kellmer Pringle' who, as the founder of the National Children's Bureau, has done more than most to bring the voice of the child into the debate about the life that child might lead. A challenge to the view that the institutions of the adult world are best able to understand the needs of the children who inhabit them.

Wells, Gordon. *The Meaning Makers*. Portsmouth, NH: Heinemann 1985. Wells's study considers how children use language both to make and to understand meaning. Using examples of recorded conversation between adults and children, he shows how the use of language develops and the purposes served by its development at home and at school. The long time span over which the children were studied (eight years in some cases) provides an interesting comparison of their development.

Wood, D. *How Children Think and Learn*. Cambridge, MA: Blackwell 1988. An overview of the work of the developmental psychologist in explaining the way that children understand the world. Work by Piaget, Vygotsky, Bruner and Chomsky is included. Most of the emphasis is on children above five.